Dear
Baby Rosenberger

May God bless you
keep you happy, he

Natalie Fried

I would like to dedicate this book to
my family and friends—
those I have known and
those I have yet to meet —
and especially to my husband and children.

In loving memory of Mimi.

May prayer be like breath.

Help Me Pray Today

by Natalie Friedl
Illustrated by Izabela Ciesinska

Halo ●●●●
Publishing International®

Help Me Pray Today
First Edition 2008
Text Copyright ©2008 Natalie Friedl
Illustrations Copyright © 2008 by Izabela Ciesinska
Library of Congress Cataloging-in-Publication Data
Editor Marlene Marchinko

ISBN 13: 978-0-9797429-1-0
ISBN 10: 0-9797429-1-9
Printed in China

Published by

Halo
Publishing International®
6415 Granger Road, Independence, OH 44131
Website: www.halopublishing.com
Telephone: (216) 255-6756

Thank you, God, for another day.
Help me live it in your way.

"I will give thanks to the Lord with all my heart;
I will tell of all your wonders."

Psalms 9:1

Thank you, God, for my hands and feet.
Help me try to keep them neat.

Purity

Thank you, God, for my eyes and ears.
Help me bravely face all my fears.

Thank you, God, for my mind.
Help me remember to be kind.

"So, as those who have been chosen of God,
holy and beloved, put on a heart of compassion,
kindness, humility, gentleness and patience."

Colossians 3:12

Thank you, God, for all my friends.
Help me learn to make amends.

"Do not judge, and you will not be judged.
Do not condemn, and you will not be condemned.
Forgive, and you will be forgiven."

Luke 6:37

Thank you, God, for a chance to pray.
Help me do it while I play.

"And all things you ask in prayer,
believing, you will receive."
Matthew 21:22

Thank you, God, for Mom and Dad.
Help me do what makes them glad.

"Honor your father and your mother,
that your days may be prolonged in the land
which the Lord your God gives you."

Exodus 20:12

Thank you, God, for the clouds and sky.
Help me watch as they go by.

"God saw all that he had made, and it was very good.
And there was evening, and there was morning – the sixth day."

Genesis 1:31

Creation

Thank you, God, for music and art.
Help me try to take a part.

"We have different gifts,
according to the grace given us."
Romans 12:6

Thank you, God, for birds and bees.
Help me care for all of these.

"The earth is the Lord's, and everything in it,
the world, and all who live in it."

Psalms 24:1

Thank you, God, for sisters and brothers.
Help me learn to share with others.

"Love each other as brothers and sisters
and honor others more than you do yourself."
Romans 12:10

Thank you, God, for my home.
Help me pray for those who roam.

"So in everything, do to others what you would have them
do to you, for this sums up the Law and the Prophets."

Matthew 7:12

Thank you, God, for memories.
Help me remember each of these.

"For where two or three have gathered together
in my name, I am there in their midst."

Matthew 18:20